THE VISITOR

GIFTS IN STRANGE WRAPPINGS

Bree Abbington

Copyright © 2014 Bree Abbington
Originally titled *The Christmas Visitor*

All rights reserved. Without limiting the rights under copyright reserved herein, no part of this publication may be reproduced, stored in or introduced into a retrieval system, or transmitted, in any form or by any means (electronic, mechanical, photocopying, recording or otherwise) without the prior written permission of the copyright owner of this book.

ISBN:0615959741
ISBN-13: 978-0615959740

DEDICATION

For my dear friend, Phyllis, who has always encouraged me to see gifts, even if they are in strange wrappings!

Table of Contents

PREFACE 1
CHAPTER 1 The Escape 2
CHAPTER 2 The Cleanup 12
CHAPTER 3 The Visitor 18
CHAPTER 4 The Rescue 23
CHAPTER 5 The Thaw Out 29
CHAPTER 6 The Gift 35
CHAPTER 7 Getting Back on Your Feet 39
CHAPTER 8 Rescue Two 41
CHAPTER 9 The Intervention 44
CHAPTER 10 After Words 48

PREFACE

The Universe is a strange and awesome place, a mystical realm bestowing gifts that are often unimaginable. In the sphere of our lives there are certain gifts we will always remember and cherish. These particular gifts seem to stay in our hearts long after we recall the date such a gift was received. Christmas is one of those magical times where we receive some of our most memorable gifts. Sometimes these gifts come in strange wrappings. Sometimes they come in no wrapping at all. Our fortune in life often resides in our ability to recognize the special nature of gifts when they are presented. Then we have to couple that recognition with wisdom and courage to discern that some gifts are indeed a magical connection to the universe we know.

CHAPTER 1
THE GREAT ESCAPE

I returned to my home on Christmas day to escape. I was a woman seeking sanctuary and a nap. I was escaping the post gift - opening and brunch mayhem of Christmas morning at my former in-laws' home. The Christmas climax had been reached. All of the gifts under the tree had been unwrapped. One new toy had already been broken. The hustle and bustle of Christmas preparations and events was behind us. The only remaining Christmas highlight was the traditional gathering for a family Christmas dinner that evening.

I was escaping ex-husband number one. Matt is a good guy and great father, but not a fan of the Christmas spirit. As often occurred during the yuletide season, he was becoming grumpy. This has developed into an unfortunate, unpleasant seasonal tradition. After 15 years of marriage and almost 5 more as a very happily divorced couple, the signs were becoming increasingly evident. To his credit Matt's grumbling seemed less pronounced as the years passed. Regrettably, there is nothing anyone can do to prevent his inevitable Christmas Day meltdown. My post-divorce tactic has been to attempt to depart before Matt starts his grousing.

I was also escaping my beloved children, Nicole and Sabrina. At their respective ages of 12 and 5, they are both adorable and fun. At least that can be said most of the time. We always look forward to Christmas break from school. It is a chance for all of us to regroup. We gather supplies for the cold, dark days of winter as we resign ourselves to the wait involved in looking for signs of spring. There comes a specific point during Christmas break every year where we all know it is time for the girls to return to school and our normal routine. Because the school vacation had started earlier than usual that year, the threshold of my parental patience and the need to return to normal life had already been crossed.

I was escaping Christmas until the appointed time for cocktail hour and the traditional Abbington Christmas dinner. I was looking forward to this, but still had the need to escape Christmas for a few hours. In part, I wanted quiet time to go home and reflect on the last year. Mainly, I just wanted to take a well-earned Christmas nap. My unexpected visitor had a different plan.

The Abbingtons have a tradition. In actuality we have many, but one is special. This tradition started when Nicole was an infant. We all spend the night at my in-laws' home. Technically, Phil and Barbara are no longer my in-laws. The term "ex-in-laws" would apply. I have always found this term awkward and inapplicable to our relationship. I divorced Matt, not them. I still love them. No one else will ever replace them in my heart. So I refer to them as my in-laws.

Our tradition of the Christmas evening sleepover has endured post-divorce. The tradition started so we could all get up in our pajamas and enjoy the delight of Christmas morning with small children. Our children don't really believe in Santa Claus, but we leave a note at our house explaining where to forward the gifts. Magically, the gifts have always found their way to the intended recipients.

Another aspect of our traditional sleepover is Christmas Eve pizza. Then, if I can talk the other adults into it, we watch *It's a Wonderful Life*. Afterwards we write a note to Santa thanking him, and leave a treat for his reindeer. We tell stories of Christmases past, and simply enjoy the warmth of family. Everyone gets to open one gift. Then it's bedtime for the children. After the re-telling of *'Twas the Night Before Christmas,* the children are safely tucked in bed and the adults spring into action. The gifts are relocated to the tree from their hiding places. We are ready for the morning.

As in millions of homes around the world, the morning

brings the raucous spectacle of sharing gifts, followed by the aromas and tastes associated with a bountiful and wonderful brunch. After a respite from the warmth of family sharing and loving excess, the culmination of the day is the Abbington family Christmas dinner. Our Christmas dinner is always wonderful. The good china makes an appearance. It is accompanied by candlelight and wonderful wine. We don't bother with music. It would merely be sacrificed to the wonderful conversations which are usually overlapping and loud. These conversations are always punctuated with laughter.

The fact that we continued these traditions after Matt and I divorced seemed strange to some people. For me it was logical. It is neutral, safe ground where everyone feels comfortable. This way neither of us has to miss Christmas morning with our girls.

Christmas is the most wonderful time of the year. It is also the most chaotic and draining season for a single mother of two. This is true under the best of circumstances. The last year had not been the best of circumstances. I was trying hard to make Christmas wonderful for my children. Needless to say, the tidings of comfort and joy were escaping me.

The preceding year had seen the explosive end of my

short-lived second marriage, health issues, legal issues, and the involuntary decision to close a once extremely profitable business that I had at one time loved. I still can't say for sure whether my legal issues caused my health issues, or my health issues caused my legal issues. The problems, both legal and health, had been chronic concerns for years.

The health issues began with the discovery of a benign tumor in my head. I have treated it for the last ten years. The tumor is gone, but the infections related to the removal persist. The years of strong antibiotics decimated my stomach and colon. This condition was made far worse by the stress of the business.

To say mistakes made in the business were minor in scope would be like saying the Titanic was unsinkable. My health and legal issues reached an acute crescendo early in the year. I had no other alternative but to close the doors. When I announced the decision to abandon ship concerning the business, my second husband Brad announced his decision to do the same regarding our marriage.

The fact that I had pulled together Christmas was a miracle. This miracle had happened in spite of my wavering second ex-husband's antics. Brad refused to turn over insurance checks reimbursing me for my many out-of-pocket medical expenses. I was depending on this money for the holidays. This hostility reminded me of my childhood affinity for *The Grinch Who Stole Christmas*. Doctor Seuss's line about the Grinch resonated with me that year, "He didn't stop Christmas from coming. Somehow or other, it came. It came just the same."

I took real satisfaction in the fact that Brad's act of economic terrorism really hadn't had any visible effect on my children's Christmas. I have a favorite scene in *The Grinch Who Stole Christmas* where the Grinch is perched high on the peak of Mount Crumpit. He pauses to hear the Whos' cries when they realize their Christmas has been stolen. To the surprise of the Grinch, the Whos begin to sing. The puzzled look on the Grinch's face is priceless. The image of Brad as the Grinch in this scene gave me great pleasure.

With the help of my generous family and Matt's family, we had pulled it together. The Christmas smiles of Nicole and Sabrina were the only evidence I needed. As a Christmas team we were flawless. It wasn't easy, but the mission was accomplished. Then again, the Abbington clan is resourceful. We are awesome at getting things done. We may squabble among ourselves, but this is a game in which outsiders are not allowed to participate. We are masters at circling the wagons. Wagon-circling is an activity in which we have a lot of experience.

Brad fulfilled the role of the Grinch as if straight from central casting. Unsurprisingly, he frowned on the Abbington family Christmas sleepover. Now that Brad was gone from my life his interference was no longer an obstacle. This was the first Christmas after his abrupt departure. I was so relieved I didn't have to justify our tradition to Brad. It had resulted in hard feelings every Christmas we were together. Last Christmas Brad's domineering personality was on ugly display as he made mocking references to the occasion and stopped just short of denying our family participation. In an attempt to salvage my sinking marriage, I had agreed not to attend the Christmas Eve sleepover. I spent most of the evening in my bathroom regretting my decision bathed in tears of anger and self-loathing.

Christmas this year had seemed comparatively anti-climactic. The prior week the landscape had glistened in a heavenly gown of wondrous white. The previous Saturday my best friend Julie had come to town to celebrate Chrismikah. This is another of my family's strange traditions. Julie is Jewish and Nicole's godmother. This is our combined Christmas and Hanukah celebration, and although the date of the celebration is irrelevant to us all, the celebration itself is an integral part of our lives and love.

THE VISITOR

Distance makes it impossible to get together with Aunt Julie twice during the month of December. Chrismikah was born out of our attempt to celebrate both holidays on one mutually convenient date. We exchange gifts. My girls get Hanukah gifts. Aunt Julie gets Christmas gifts We play dreidels in front of the Christmas tree. We dispense with the singing of both Christmas and Hanukah songs in favor of whatever is on our iTunes play list. We tell inappropriately funny stories. The tales are from our past. The best are about how Julie, Matt and I all met in graduate school over 20 years ago. Some of these stories have taken on a life of their own. They probably have very little resemblance to what happened, but we enjoy them.

This year was the best Chrismikah ever! It was 24 hours packed absolutely full of activity. The snowy landscape made for the perfect setting. The thermometer climbed steadily all day. In the afternoon, the temperature got up to 65 degrees. We played outside in the snow without jackets. The Arctic chill that had been with us for a week had left thick ice on our pond. The warm weather had ruined the ice for skating, but it was still solid enough for play. As the sun went down, the wine appeared. The winter evening was filled with cooking, baking and all kinds of merriment.

The next day, unfortunately, our white Christmas was no

more. The Christmas week errands were largely done in the rain. This didn't help anyone's spirits. The bell ringers outside Macy's usually look so happy. As I entered the mall, the gentleman on bell-ringing-duty just looked tortured.

On Christmas Eve, the girls and I darted around the house like maniacs making the final Christmas preparations. We had elected to skip Christmas Eve church services which had also been a long standing tradition in our family. I justified this to the girls by telling them that we had simply run out of time. Nicole gave me a questioning look with a raised eyebrow which resembled mine. She looked stunning in her Christmas dress, and had spent about an hour on her hair. She is a smart girl. She had the wisdom to let it go.

The last pre-departure activity was to take the traditional Christmas pictures in front of the tree. Sabrina was not cooperating. These antics are also a Christmas tradition. After I got a passable picture we darted out the door. We left the wreckage of last minute Christmas preparations in our wake, and headed for Phil and Barbara's home.

Finally, the errands, preparations, and Christmas morning chaos were done. We had managed another awesome Christmas. There weren't many gifts for me this year, but that was all right. The only gift I wanted was to slip home from my in-laws, clean up the pre-Christmas debris field, and take a nap before getting ready for dinner. I also knew I needed a few minutes to myself. I had prepared 20 teachers' gifts and turned the proverbial two loaves and five fish into a feast. A nap really didn't sound like a huge request.

I explained this to my in-laws. They graciously agreed. This would give them additional time with Nicole and Sabrina. Phil and Barbara have reached the age that they have earned the right to flee south and escape the worst part of the northeast winter. The following week they were leaving for the warmth of a southern island for a month.

With the blessings of my in-laws, I exited quietly while the girls played with their Christmas morning bounty. Our dogs, Yip and Yap, ran around in matching Santa costumes. The last thing I wanted was the children or dogs to see my departure, or there would be no nap time for me. Still in my Christmas pajamas, I traveled the five mile distance to my home. I struggled to keep my eyes open.

CHAPTER 2

THE CLEANUP

My exit went undetected by the children and the dogs. A short time later, I pulled the SUV into the garage of my home.

A brief aside, those are words I love – "My home." Brad and I had lived there together during our ill-fated 18 month marriage, but we never quite got around to adding him to the deed. In the wake of his departure, very few things gave me solace as much as the words, "My home." Upon the advice of my therapist, I hadn't decided if the girls and I would stay there. It was large. The financial and physical upkeep made staying an improbable idea. I was only waiting for enough distance make a rational decision. All professional recommendations were to wait a year. It was unimaginable, but I was almost there.

I was still in my pajamas and Uggs. I am so glad that I had not been stopped for any traffic infractions on the way

THE VISITOR

home still in my pajamas. Matt is a public official. I try hard not to embarrass him or the rest of my family. Over the last year, I had totally failed in this mission. My business and legal issues had played out on the front pages of the local papers. I often feel our community may be one of the few places left where people still read the local paper. I had to give the alert of incoming media coverage to family and close friends too many times over the past year.

I feel blessed that most of these people still talk to me and care about me. In a crisis some people leave and some people stay. For some people friendship becomes an observation sport. They are waiting around mainly to see how the story ends. They offer encouragement and support, but this is done from the safe distance of the sidelines. The special friends rush in grab the hose and help you try to put out the fire. The special ones do this even when your negligence lit the fire   I am lucky to have a lot of these special people in my life. I am trying very hard to do better, and not attract media attention. I was giving passing thought to making that my New Year's resolution.

I had only one real thought on my mind – prioritization. Within the next four hours, I needed to nap, shower, dress for dinner, and clean the house just a little. What should I do first? For a single mom who is used to multi-page task lists, this was doable. The freedom to prioritize these tasks in the absence of Nicole and Sab was a double blessing. I love my children dearly, but I get things done far quicker when they are not home. The house was extra quiet without the company of Yip and Yap. I am a big dog fan. These dogs are miniatures. Their names reflect their favorite pastime. They bark at everything, which makes napping with them in the house difficult if not impossible.

As I mentally prioritized, a nap was leading the list. I walked into the house, and threw the car keys on the counter. Silence reigned. The carnage of the Christmas Eve preparations was even worse than I remembered. My better judgment said to at least close the cabinet doors and begin to pick-up the scraps of wrapping paper and such off the floor. While I was at it, why not throw in a load of laundry?

In the back of my mind lingered a fourth goal – no tears. It would have been far too easy to sit and mourn the Christmases past. Hot on the heels of my separation from Matt, Brad had swept into my world. He was tall, dark, handsome, and well educated with impeccable manners. Matt is many terrific things. Refined is not included on that list. Brad was the definition of refined. At least he was on the surface. He is the type of man who owns a tuxedo, and likes to wear it.

In the early part of our courtship he was truly wonderful. I had never felt so cared for or adored. When my business failed and it was clear that there were several impending disasters on the horizon, he was the first one out the door. Having someone pledge his undying commitment and abandon you 18 months later as soon as the prospect of trouble emerged hurts. "Hurts" isn't actually strong enough: it cuts to the core. Matt takes pride in being the only one who saw through the charade of my tuxedo-clad suitor from the beginning. I was left in shock. My friends and my family were in disbelief.

During our relationship and brief marriage, Brad and I made every effort to make Christmas extra special for our combined family. We each had two daughters who had been through the trauma of divorce and loss. We had huge Christmas trees. Family and friends gathered. We enjoyed movie nights, and played the game with the evil-looking Elf on the Shelf. We would play wonderful Christmas music, cook together, and laugh as a happy family.

Combining families is always hard. Children cling to the family traditions of their birth families. We tried to balance old traditions and new. I hate the term "blended family." It implies that everyone gets all chopped up in a kitchen device with sharp blades. A caring friend shared a better term to describe combining families "a crockpot family." Everything goes in one pot and slowly simmers. No one is forced to give up his or her original form. The flavors combine slowly to create something delicious. Our goal from the start was to be a crockpot family. It wasn't always perfect. There were many squabbles, territory wars, and one outright brawl, but I thought we were happy.

The fairytale all ended with the words, "I have decided to leave." This five word sentence rocked my world. The sentence can be better translated as, "The gravy train is about to end. This is about to get ugly, and I am gone." This was the first time that I had ever truly had my heart broken. Almost a year later, it still stings like a fresh wound on some days. My friends and family have been great about supporting me and encouraging me. After the divorce several of my friends have done what can only be described as a modern day shunning of Brad. As an educated person raised in a family who always went to church, I get that is wrong in most of the world's modern religions and certainly my own, but I can't say I have done anything to actively dissuade them.

All I really wanted was to take my nap, clean my house, get ready for the traditional Abbington Christmas dinner, and not have a complete crying fit. Again, none of these desires seemed like a huge request.

CHAPTER 3

THE VISITOR

So, like the Cat at the end of *The Cat in the Hat*, I began to get things back to normal around the house. I was happy just to have a few hours to catch my breath before Christmas dinner. I looked around doing a housekeeping triage. I cleaned up a few of the more glaring messes. I put away the ketchup bottle which was still on the counter from Nicole's snack the evening before. I put the dishes in the dishwasher. Most of the litter was removed from the floor of the living room. It wasn't what anyone would consider tidy, but I could live with it.

At that point, my bed beckoned. I had spent the previous evening in a double bed with Nicole. Anyone who has ever spent a night in bed with her calls her the "Washing Machine." It is a title well earned. On several occasions, I have awoken with Nicole's foot in my face. One time her toe was literally in my ear. To add to the Christmas Eve entertainment, the alarm clock in the guest room where we spent the night went off at midnight for no reason. I tried desperately to silence it before it set off Yip and Yap, who were across the hall with Matt and Sabrina. I finally unplugged it. I lay in bed all night wondering what time it was. Another Abbington family tradition, the children aren't allowed to get up until there is at least some sign of daylight. It was a very long night! My eyes were burning.

I headed toward my bedroom and my empty king size bed. I was ready for some rest. I was physically and mentally tired to the bone. I gazed out the window at the stark, snowless landscape. The pond behind our home is large. In past winters, it has been the center of all types of ice skating sports. You have not lived until you have seen what passes for the girl version of ice hockey. Last winter, as my marriage to Brad imploded, the pond never froze. There was never a layer of ice which merited checking to see if it was thick enough to use safely. With the chill that had descended on my marriage and the household, the warm winter and lack of ice on the pond seemed almost comical. We never lit one fire in the fire pit on the bank of the pond.

I had been hoping for a white winter, and a return to the pond. Playing on the pond on Chrismikah the week before had been a partial return to what passes as normal around my home. The pre-Christmas rain had deteriorated the condition of the ice in the week since Chrismikah. I studied the ice from the warmth of my bedroom. There were parts of the ice where open water was visible. This is never a good sign. The temperature over the last few days had fallen. If the cold snap continued, we would have skating ice without a doubt. I considered the possibility of a skating party before the Christmas break ended.

It was then that I saw it. At first, I wanted to say that it was just my imagination and not really there. I was tired. My vision was blurry. Could I be hallucinating? I wanted rest so badly. I blinked, and rubbed my eyes. There was no denying it. Sticking up between the cattails, there was something that didn't belong. There were two ears.

What was it? The neighbors have a large dog, but these ears were too big to belong to the neighbor's dog. Even if Yip and Yap had been home, it was too big to be either of them. It didn't take my tired brain long to figure out – it was the deer.

Not a deer, but the deer.

I grew up in Pennsylvania. Hunting is so popular there that the schools actually are closed on the first day of hunting season. Matt is an incredible hunter. It is not a sport in which I have ever had any wish to engage, but I am very familiar with it because I have been around it my whole life.

The Abbington girls have likewise been around hunting their whole lives. During my ill-fated second marriage, one evening as we pulled into the driveway we saw several deer grazing in our large yard. The deer gave our car only a passing glance. They didn't leave. My step-child said, "Look! They like us." Nicole immediately responded in a deadpan tone, "No, they just know that no one in this house owns a gun."

The girls and I had often seen this little deer before in the yard. This drives Yip and Yap into a state of frenzy. She became a frequent guest in our yard right after the start of doe season. It wasn't hard to figure out the story behind our visitor. We had a real life Bambi on our hands.

During the fall, she would just lay in our yard. I would pull in or out of the driveway in the car, and she would just look at me. This abnormal animal behavior only happens in the movies. One day, mainly out of curiosity and because I wasn't in my normal rush, I got out of the car and walked toward her. There was absolutely nothing wrong with this little doe. She instantly ran as only a deer can. She was back in the safety of the woods in seconds.

On a couple of occasions, I will admit I let Nicole and Sabrina put some apples out for her. This practice would have been frowned upon by any wildlife management expert and Matt. This was a wild animal, and any attempt to interact or tame her would end badly. Even I understand this; however, it didn't take much for the girls to convince me to allow them to serve appetizers to the deer. This deer seemed to come around whether it was fed or not. I had often spotted her down on the bank of the pond getting a drink and grazing on the acorns.

This time she was not in the yard or drinking from the pond. She was two feet out on the semi-frozen pond. She was lying on the ice just looking at the house like this was the most natural thing in the world.

CHAPTER 4
THE RESCUE

So did I mention I really wanted a nap? I understood fully the importance of what was happening. No deer would ever just lie down on the ice to take a nap or rest, not even this semi-tame creature. This deer had fallen down on the ice, and was not getting up. That could mean only one thing - she couldn't get up by herself. Unless I did something, I would have a dead deer on my pond. The thought of this was bad on so many levels. We had come to really enjoy watching the deer in our yard. I would have to explain to Nicole and Sabrina why their favorite deer friend was dead on the pond on Christmas. The thought of that caused me to let out an audible groan.

Ultimately, I would have to beg Matt or someone else to come get the corpse. This would probably also entail enduring a lecture from Matt about my folly in letting the kids feed it in the first place. Matt doesn't do it as often as I probably deserve it, but he is great at the art of telling you "I told you so," without actually using those words. I'm not sure if this is a gift or a talent. I am sure I didn't want to be on the receiving end of it yet again especially on Christmas day.

I looked longingly at my bed, but I knew that was a choice I couldn't live with. So, back to the laundry room I went to find my outside gear. While certainly not the coldest Christmas on record, it was only in the 20's. I opted for my ski coat and pants. I had to rummage, but eventually I found them, along with my ski gloves.

I suited up and headed for the pond. I really had no clear idea in my head what I was going to do. I mainly went to assess the situation. As I approached, it was clear this deer couldn't get up under her own power. For a second, the angle made it appear her legs were through the ice. I let out a small prayer when I realized this wasn't the case. She was just lying with her legs under her.

I made my way cautiously out onto the ice. There were lots of cracking noises under my Uggs, but the ice showed no real sign of giving. I tested the ice very cautiously at first. As the writer Anne Lamont says, "You can't test courage cautiously." After all, the deer was on the shallow end of the pond. If I went through the ice, I would be wet and standing in water up to my knees. I am not sure that the Uggs would recover from that, but I would. After everything else I had been through this year, my thought was, "Oh well." There is an interesting thing about damaged people. In some ways they are dangerous because they are willing to take risks others might avoid. They have learned a valuable life lesson – they may get wet and ruin their shoes, but they will survive.

Out onto the ice I went to greet my surprise visitor. As I approached, the deer just watched me. Deer have the most incredible eyes. They are huge, deep brown, intelligent looking, and penetrating when they study something. This deer was studying me. There wasn't any concern in her eyes. Her eyes showed no panic or fear of me or the situation. She just watched me walk awkwardly across the ice toward her. It almost felt like she was expecting me.

When I reached her, I bent over and put my hand out like one would do when approaching a dog for the first time. Okay, I realize this sounds silly, but it was just my instinct. I spoke to her softly. Then I felt the complete insanity of having asked this creature how she was. When the deer did not flinch, I petted her head. My house is a house of girls. Even Yip and Yap are girls. My house of girls had always assumed that this was a doe. To my surprise, we were wrong. It was button buck. That was unexpected. A button buck is a young buck that hasn't yet fully developed antlers. Buried beneath its beautiful brown fur between his large ears were two nubs that hopefully someday would get the chance to be a full rack of antlers.

I looked over the scene. There was a thin layer of snow on most of the ice. It was clear from the pattern in the snow that he had been here for a while and had been struggling to get up. He was alert. His eyes were clear and his ears at attention. I don't know much about animal care, but I understand that I had to get him off the ice as quickly as possible. But how?

I am not sure that I have ever touched a deer other than maybe at a petting zoo. This is not my area of expertise. I briefly considered returning to the house and consulting Google. That just seemed silly under the circumstances. The comic thought of the search, "How do I get a deer off the ice?" made me laugh.

He was about my size. Carrying him to the edge just seemed like a bad idea. I thought back to high school physics. The memories were very murky at best. Physics was not a stellar subject for me. I have worked hard to suppress those memories. They may add new oceans and take away Pluto in other disciplines, but the laws of physics don't change. Honestly, the fact that the laws of physics don't change is one of the few things I remember from that class. I also remember the surface of ice has little resistance and there would be little friction. Granted my terminology is probably wrong, but it made sense at the time. My decision was to first push him to the edge of the pond first.

I had no idea what I would do from there, but getting to the edge of the pond seemed like a good idea. I circled across the ice behind the deer. As I walked my awkward ice walk, I continued to reassure him that I thought this was the best idea. I was probably trying to convince myself more than the deer. I bent over, and planted my hands firmly on his rear hunches. He gave no resistance. I shoved for all I was worth. All went according to plan. The next part was going to be a little harder. I needed to get him off the pond. He was almost as big as me. What to do?

We had been fortunate to have a Labrador Retriever, Roxy. He lived to be 14. Roxy was the child before we had children. Unlike Yip and Yap he was just about my weight. In his later years, occasionally he would need a boost to get up. By the end, we would often have to lift him. This was not easy for me, but I could. A brief sadness washed over me. I really miss Roxy. He had been a great dog. Now was not the time for tears. I decided there was only one way to solve this problem. I was going to have to lift the young buck off the ice. I bent down, and picked him up much like I had done for Roxy so many times. He let out a sound like the bleating of a sheep. This also was an unexpected surprise! I didn't know deer made any noise. The shock of the noise caused me to drop him.

I recovered from my shock. The deer looked at me. If he could speak, I am sure he would have said, "What did you do that for?" I got in position to try again. I picked him up from the ice. I hefted him onto the bank of my pond. I lay down beside him on the cold, hard ground. I had been tired when I got home. I was now exhausted from the effort. We were both okay. We were tired, but off the ice and safe so far.

CHAPTER 5
THE THAW OUT

Having now accomplished my first deer ice rescue, my next thought was, "Now what do I do?" I got up and brushed myself off.

The only prudent thought that I had was to examine the deer. If he had a broken leg this was going to end very badly. I did the best I could to check him over. Nothing seemed broken. This was good. I called Matt and explained the situation. Realizing the whole thing sounded insane, I tried to keep the tone of my voice calm. While his tone was not unfriendly, it was pretty clear he had no interest in coming out in the cold to assist with my mission. His suggestion was to leave him alone. Matt made it clear. The only way he was coming over was if the deer needed to be dispatched. The thought of that made me cringe.

My next message was to my friend Jason who is also an avid outdoorsman. The text I fired off sounded insane,

"Merry Christmas. I have this issue, what do you recommend?" He was kind, but echoed Matt's words, "Leave it alone. He is a wild creature. He knows what to do, and if he doesn't or can't that's how nature works." I didn't find much solace there.

I looked at my helpless friend. I knew what Matt and Jason were saying was right, but it simply wasn't acceptable to me. Granted, my first aid skills are pathetic. Just ask Nicole and Sab. On several occasions, Nicole has sought medical attention from the mom next door. I am blessed with keen logical skills. If this were a person who had been on the ice, the first thing you would do was raise their body temperature to stop hypothermia. There was no way I was going to be able to get this guy to the house. Even if I could, I knew it that was a really bad idea. Next best solution – blankets. Off to the house I went to collect some blankets. By now all thoughts of my Christmas nap were gone.

When I returned with the blankets, I had hoped the deer would just get up and scamper away. No such luck. I covered him with two of the blankets. I placed a third on the ground beside him, and sat down and reflected.

What a year it had been. So much had happened since last Christmas. Most of it was my own fault. To say that

THE VISITOR

Brad and I had been "happy" last Christmas would be a fabrication. The marriage was already coming apart at the poorly sewn seams, but we had been together. I thought our problems were resolvable. Obviously, the incentive structure for him to stay wasn't there. I really can't blame him. If I would have had the option, I may have left me too. I had become too high maintenance for anyone to endure. My life was a train wreck in progress. It was apparent that the body-count was going to be substantial.

The year had been a financial, legal, and health disaster for me. I was in many ways caught in the perfect storm. Again, I am not saying I hadn't brought most of it upon myself, but I was beginning to feel a little like the Pharaoh in the story of Moses and the Exodus. I also identified a lot with Job, but again most of my issues were of my own making.

So here I was on Christmas day, sitting beside my pond petting a deer. I looked at my friend. I was mildly amused how much a deer and a donkey resemble each other, especially the ears. There are so many great Bible stories involving donkeys. Of course there are none involving whitetail deer. I looked up to the heavens. I certainly believe there is a God. I believe this even on the hard days. I may believe it more on the hard days. Everything and everyone comes into our lives for a reason. Some people stay a lifetime. Others are there only for a season, but they are always there for a reason. I believe that God always knows what we need and when we need it. Apparently He felt I needed to spend Christmas day rescuing a deer. The thought seemed slightly absurd, but I learned a long time ago not to question God. Just do what He is obviously asking you to do.

I began to pray. "God, hi it's me again. Sorry about that whole not making church thing last night. I know it was wrong. It was particularly wrong not to make sure the girls got there. I still believe in You and love You, but church hurts too much right now." That was the one good thing Brad and I consistently did together. We worshiped as a couple and as a family. The thought of being at Christmas Eve services without him was just too painful.

"You and I both know there is no way I would have made it through the candle light singing of *Silent Night* at church without going to pieces. I know this is a pathetic excuse, but my children have seen me cry far too often this year. If the tears would have started, I worry if I would ever have been able to get them to stop. I will try to do better, but no promises right now on the church thing."

"Thank you God for all the good things in my life.

Thank you for all the good lessons the bad things in my life have taught me this year. Thank You for the incredible strength You have given me to survive all of this. Thank You for the gifts of faith and hope. I have no idea how I am going to get through all of this, but I have faith I will. I know You hold my girls and me in Your hand and we are safe in Your care. At every turn, You have given me all I need exactly when I need it. You are amazing! Thank you for Your grace. I know Your will won't take me where Your grace can't protect me"

"So, I understand this deer is here for a reason, and that You sent it. I get I have no right to ask you for anything more because You have given me so much and so many blessings. By the way, this one is really strange. Please God, let this little guy live. I know he is hurt, alone and scared, but give him the strength and courage to live. I don't know why God, but I need this one. Yes, I get that is really unfair to ask of You with all else that goes on not just in my life but in the world. I need him to live. *Please?*"

As I said my "Amen," I realized the deer was looking at me like I was a completely cracked lunatic. The tears were flowing like a river down my face. I quickly looked around to make sure the neighbors hadn't caught sight of all this. I felt that perhaps I was making the deer a little uncomfortable.

Matt and Jason were right. I needed to give my visitor a little alone time. I realized the deer was probably on the ice in the first place trying to get a drink of water. I brought a bowl of water from the house. I also brought him some of Yip and Yap's food. It was the best I could come up with at the time. I certainly was not going to call Matt or Jason again and ask what I should feed the deer. After I placed the food and water where my visitor could easily get it, I returned to the house to wait it out. There certainly would be no nap in my future that Christmas day.

CHAPTER 6
THE GIFT

Inside, my first task was to thaw out my chilled body. I lit the fireplace, and got an uncharacteristic third cup of coffee. My limit is normally one. I had enjoyed two cups as we lingered over Christmas morning brunch. Given the morning I was having, I had no trouble justifying the third one. I sipped it sitting on the couch keeping a vigilant watch on my patient by the pond. He didn't look to be in distress, but he also showed no signs of a willingness to get up and run into the woods behind the pond.

I continued to send silent prayers up to God that this would end well. I watched for any sign that the young buck was going to get up and move. I found it absurd that my eyes were dry now. It was like the spigot had been turned off after my good cry at the pond. This last year has been one of total transition and transformation for me. Again, a lot of it was not of my choice, but as a result of my actions.

In a crisis, or in my case multiple, simultaneous crises, lots of people are quick to leave. Brad wasn't the only one to abandon me. Good friends stick by you. As I have said before, great friends march into the flames, find the hose, put out the fire, and offer to help with the clean-up. I have been so lucky to have a few such people in my life. I turned my attention to them for a few minutes. I had managed to get an incredible picture of the deer laying under a blue blanket. Against the backdrop of the barren pond, the contrast was striking. I texted the special people in my life the incredible picture that I managed to take of the deer along with a Merry Christmas message.

Over the last year I have gained a true appreciation for good friends and my family. Even on the darkest days, it is like they have formed this safety net around me. Whatever I have asked, no matter how strange, they have helped. They have endured numerous crying jags, rants, and endless babbling about my woes. They have been kind enough to let me babble. They have been even kinder when they have insisted I stop obsessing before I put my health further at risk. They have been kind as the as the local paper reported the details of my legal woes. I am sure they have been asked uncomfortable and awkward questions by those not in my inner circle. They have been gracious enough to not tell me.

For me, helping my Christmas visitor was just passing on the gift my family and true friends had given me over the last year. They had given me the gifts of unconditional love, kindness, support and understanding in abundance. As I sent up prayers for the deer, I realized how many prayers had probably been said for my girls and me over the course of the last year. I was in awe. Regardless of your faith or where you are on your personal journey, prayer is an incredible thing. Here I was on Christmas Day, after what will hopefully go down as the hardest year of my life, smiling at the thought that I got the privilege to help this deer. None of my problems were fully resolved, but they seemed inconsequential to the task at hand.

After I finished my coffee, I decided to fold some laundry while I continued to monitor the deer from the warmth of the house. As I watched, he began to move. I felt like a parent who was watching a child try to take his first steps. I let him struggle for a few minutes. Eventually, it was clear that he wanted to stand up, but couldn't. My thought, "sometimes in life all we need is for someone to give us a little boost." I grabbed my coat and gloves. I considered my other winter clothes. I thought, "This is only going to take a minute. No need for all of that." I exited the house. I was headed back for the pond bank and the deer.

CHAPTER 7
GETTING BACK ON YOUR FEET

By the time I reached the pond I was cold. I was already regretting my decision not to put on more winter clothes. The temperature had begun to fall. The deer again allowed me to approach without much fuss. Now was the moment of truth. If he couldn't get up and walk, I was going to have to make that call to Matt that I had been dreading all day. I informed the deer of this. I am not sure how, but the look in those beautiful eyes indicated to me that he got it. Get up or there is a man with a gun on speed dial.

Thoughts of Roxy in old age again went through my mind. I went behind the deer. I put my hands under his belly and lifted. Indeed, a little boost was all he needed. He was up on his feet. Everything appeared to be in working order. He stood for what seemed to be a very long time. Then he did it. He took the first tentative step, and then another. He was going to be okay.

I uttered a huge thank you to God, and smiled. Again

there were tears, but they were the good kind. I realized how long it had been since I had cried happy tears. I thanked God for this also. I told the deer that it was time to say goodbye, but that I would love seeing him around the yard and by the pond. I picked up the discarded blankets. I turned toward the house. From the view of the pond, it looked warm and inviting. I even gave myself the privilege of a "job well done" thought as I walked up the yard.

As I neared the house, I turned toward the tree-line to take one last look at the deer as he entered the woods behind my house. He wasn't there. For a brief second I wondered if I had dreamt all of this. Was I really that exhausted? Had the last year taken that much of a toll on my mind? I scanned the yard in the other direction. There was no sign of him. I was baffled. Then I spotted him. He was back on the pond. This time he was on the deep end where the ice was not nearly as thick. He had fallen again, and was looking at me expectantly for help.

CHAPTER 8
RESCUE TWO

At that point, I will admit the thought that went through my mind was, "You're kidding me God. Really?" That was quickly followed by, "Is this deer suicidal or just dim-witted?"

I considered running into the house for more clothing. I realized there was no time. The deer was laying 20 feet away from open water. I also realized that if I was going to save this guy I had to do it quickly. Not only was he on the deep end of the pond, which never freezes as quickly or as solidly, but he was about five feet out, not two or three. It is one thing to walk out on ice where it is only two feet deep. This was whole different situation. My guess is the water where the deer had fallen this time was about eight feet deep. I couldn't even mentally calculate how thin that ice probably was. My stomach went into knots. In addition to being bad at first-aid and physics, I am not what anyone would consider a great swimmer.

My thought as I took the first tentative step out on the

pond was, "Okay God. I got it. I know what You want me to do." The thought of Jonah and the whale flashed through my mind. Like Jonah and God's wish for him to travel to Nineveh, I wanted to go anywhere but out on that ice. A sickening sound of crack came up from the ice. Clearly not a good spot for my entry. I quickly jumped back to the bank. I went toward the shallow end of the pond. I found a spot where the ice was a little thicker. I tried it again. The ice held. I held my breath. One step and then the next. I saw the small little cracks starting to emerge in the glossy ice. None of them were too threatening, but still not reassuring.

I reached the deer. This time without hesitation or conversation, I pushed his hindquarters for all I was worth. His slide across the ice looked like Thumper in the original movie *Bambi*. My one shove got him clear to the bank. I moved in that direction quickly. It was clear the ice here was thin. Very thin. In life you never know how strong you are, until strong is all you've got. I heard the splitting of the ice. I quickly grabbed the deer and threw him to the bank and jumped to safety, almost landing on him as the ice gave way. I had managed to rescue him again. My heart was pounding in my chest. This time the deer immediately stood up. His look was quizzical. If he had the power of speech, again I'm sure his question would have been, "What did you do that

THE VISITOR

for?" My intentions were good, but my actions were not gentle.

I got to my feet and told the deer in no uncertain terms that he was not allowed to go back out on the ice, even if it was the quickest route to the woods. The response I got was much like when I speak to one of my children when the television is on. The deer was looking right past me at the ice. He clearly was not listening and he was up for attempt number three. Dear God!

CHAPTER 9
THE INTERVENTION

During the course of my life I have had the "privilege" of being involved in several interventions for family and close friends who were hell bent on the path of self-destruction. Given the last year of my life, I have also been the recipient of lots of good therapy and counseling. Even on my darkest days, I have never thought about hurting myself. Mainly because I have seen what happens when people do, and the effect on all the people they leave behind. Suicide is a bad permanent solution to temporary problems even if you are a confused deer.

Never in my wildest dreams would I have imagined having to do an intervention alone with a deer with suicidal tendencies on Christmas Day. I know the suicide rate skyrockets around the holidays, but this deer couldn't possibly know that statistic. Again, I do firmly believe that God puts you where He wants you in life, but this was a stretch.

THE VISITOR

Evening was approaching. As the sun started to go down, so did the temperature. If I went into the house to grab more clothes, my visitor would be back on the ice. It probably wouldn't hold his weight now. I was sure a third rescue wasn't possible even if I was willing. So I did all I could think to do. I started a monologue. Having talked people out of hurting themselves before, I fully understand the best way to do this is to get them talking and keep them talking. Not an easy task when you have a deer on the other end of the conversation. This was going to be a very one-sided conversation.

The deer and I were facing each other. He clearly wanted to go back out on the pond and was looking for a way to get around me. I didn't get the sense that he was strong enough yet to dart. So I talked, and he listened. I talked about how even though bad things happen in life, life is still a gift. I took a step toward him. He backed away from the pond a step, but he was still looking at it intently.

I talked about how people leave, sometimes even when we desperately want them to stay. I took two more steps toward him. We were almost toe to toe. He took two steps back away from the pond.

I talked about the people who do love you, and will love

you, no matter how badly you mess up in life. I took a giant step toward him. He took one back, and one to the left toward the woods. Now his eyes were totally fixed on me and not the pond.

I talked about how sometimes it all has to fall apart so something better can fall together. I took another step toward him. He took two toward the woods. He was still listening

I talked about the fact that bad things happen in life, so we can learn and grow and become the people God wants us to be. I took another step toward him. He took three toward the woods.

This went on for the better part of an hour. I told the deer all of the wonderful, painful lessons I learned over the last year. His eyes never left mine as gently we moved step by step together until he reached the safety of the woods. When we were there I stopped talking. There was more that I could have said. I was amazed at how much I had learned and how I had grown over the last year. Until I started to tell this lost deer about it, I had not realized it myself. It was time for him to return to his home, and for me to return to my family. We stared at each other a very long time. His beautiful large ears twitched. It felt like he wanted me to keep talking. I didn't say another word. Finally he turned and bounded into the

THE VISITOR

woods like he had never been hurt. I looked on and smiled.

CHAPTER 10
AFTER WORDS

I did make it to the traditional Abbington family Christmas dinner that evening. I never did get my shower, but I did get changed. Yes I showed up wearing something other than my Christmas pajamas that I had been in all day. But I mean something more.

For a seed to grow into a plant, the seed itself goes through a metamorphosis that results in its destruction of the once seed. If this doesn't happen, there will never be a plant only just the seed of what could be a plant. For me that has been what my last year has been about. I have not fully grown into the plant that I feel I am intended to be. It took the gift of my Christmas visitor to make me step outside myself and realize that the last year hasn't been just about destruction. It has also been about creation. It has been about finding and becoming something so much better than the seed I once was.

THE VISITOR

I told my family the story over our family dinner on the good china with our wine and candlelight. Nicole and Sabrina protested that I hadn't had their father bring them out to help me. I explained that there are some times in life when you have to go it alone. This had been one of them.

When my head hit the pillow that evening, I fell into the most peaceful sleep I have had in a year. It was part the exhaustion of the day, the season, and the whole year, but there was more to my solid slumber. It was sense of knowing I had made a difference. So many people have helped me so much on my journey. The ability to give back in a meaningful way was more powerful than any sleeping pill ever created. I had wonderful dreams about my Christmas gift and what both he and I would grow into being.

www.ingramcontent.com/pod-product-compliance
Lightning Source LLC
Chambersburg PA
CBHW051717040426
42446CB00008B/935